Exploring Mars

D J Ward

LERNER BOOKS ◆ LONDON ◆ NEW YORK ◆ MINNEAPOLIS

To Lincoln - Mars awaits!

Thank you, Alane Ferguson, for twisting my arm. Thanks also to Jennifer Heldmann, Carol Stoker, Jeffrey Plaut, David Senske and Michael Malin for your helpful interviews. .

First published in the United Kingdom in 2008 by
Lerner Books,
Dalton House,
60 Windsor Avenue,
London SW19 2RR

Website address: www.lernerbooks.co.uk

This edition was updated and edited for UK publication by Discovery Books Ltd.,
Unit 3, 37 Watling Street, Leintwardine, Shropshire SY7 0LW

British Library Cataloguing in Publication Data

Ward, David J. (David John), 1966-
  Exploring Mars. - (Cool science)
  1. Mars (Planet) - Juvenile literature
  I. Title
  523.4'3

  ISBN-13: 978 1 58013 421 7

Printed in China

Table of Contents

Introduction

You are frozen to the spot. A hideous creature with gleaming eyes stares in your direction. Saliva drips from its quivering mouth. Its tentacles reach towards you. Your eyes grow wide. You hold your breath. Should you run? Should you scream? Or should you just turn off the TV?

Martians have attacked us in our nightmares. They have blasted us to smithereens in movies. In real life, though, no Martian has ever been to Earth.

Could it be that not even Mars has Martians? Probes and rovers from Planet Earth have explored the hills and valleys of Mars. They found no aliens waiting to greet us. That doesn't necessarily mean nobody's home. Life may be thriving on Mars somewhere beneath the surface.

Mars is an obvious place to look for neighbours. Like Earth, Mars has ice caps, seasons and an atmosphere. In many other ways, it is so alien.

FLYING SAUCERS HAVE
INVADED OUR PLANET...
WASHINGTON, LONDON,
PARIS, MOSCOW
FIGHT BACK!

EARTH vs. THE FLYING SAUCERS

HUGH MARLOWE · JOAN TAYLOR
with DONALD CURTIS

On the surface are features as bizarre as any Hollywood Martian. The planet has volcanoes bigger than any on Earth. It has a canyon nearly as long

Films such as Earth vs the Flying Saucers (1956) capture the human fascination with life from other worlds – often Mars.

as the Grand Canyon in the United States. Countless craters from the impact of space rocks dot the surface. These features tell us Mars was once very different. It was more active, much wetter and perhaps more alive.

Soon Mars may be invaded by aliens from another planet – human beings! Plans are under way to send humans there in our lifetimes. Some hope we won't just visit. They want to turn this cold and dusty planet into a future home for the human race.

What made Mars the way it is? Does life exist on Mars? Can we live there? We are rapidly finding answers to these questions. Faster than ever before, our red neighbour is giving up its secrets.

chapter 1

The Red Planet

Mars is the fourth planet from the Sun – just one past Earth. Viewed without a telescope, Mars is simply a red dot in the night sky. If you didn't know better, you'd think it was a star. Its true identity as a planet is revealed when you track its motion. Stars are locked into their constellation patterns, but planets drift from one constellation to another as the year goes by.

Mars is the fourth planet from the Sun. Its nearest neighbour is the Earth. Because of its rusty colour many people call it the red planet.

The Moons of Mars

Mars has two moons. One is named Phobos and the other is Deimos. Phobos and Deimos aren't much to look at. The Earth's moon is big, white and round — very impressive. The moons of Mars are tiny, brown and shaped like potatoes. Phobos, the bigger of the two, is only about 20 kilometres (13 miles) across. The moons' size and shape indicate

The moons of Mars — Phobos (above) and Deimos — are small and oddly shaped.

they probably started out as asteroids. Asteroids are space rocks that orbit the Sun but are too small to be considered planets. Most of them are in the space between Mars and Jupiter. This zone of space rocks is called the asteroid belt. Phobos and Deimos were probably captured by Mars's gravity as they drifted past.

Small and Red

Compared to the Earth, Mars is quite small. It is only a little more than half as wide as our planet. Because of its smaller size, Mars has only about one-third of the gravitational pull of Earth. Imagine if a person weighing 45 kilograms took their bathroom scales to Mars. On Mars the scale would read only about 17 kg. Want to lose weight without ever going on a diet? Go to Mars!

The 'red planet' looks red because it is rusty. Martian soil is full of iron. Much of the iron has rusted, giving the planet its red colour. Windstorms toss tonnes of this rusty dust into the air, colouring the sky pink.

IT'S A FACT!
Some Martian windstorms are big enough to cover half the planet at once!

The Planet of War

Red is the colour of blood and rage. Perhaps because of its 'angry' colour, many ancient people associated Mars (*below*) with war. Some watched the movement of Mars in the sky for news about the future. They thought it might predict victory in battle or send warning of defeat. The name *Mars* comes from the ancient Romans' name for their god of war.

Cold, Thirsty and (Almost) Airless

Mars is a very cold place. The average temperature on Mars is −55°C. Temperatures during a Martian summer day can reach 27°C, but the warmth doesn't last. Mars's nights are often more than 56°C colder than its days. With conditions like these, water can't stay liquid on the Martian surface. Space probes and landers have found water, ice and water vapour (water as a gas) on Mars. No liquid water has ever been detected there.

Mars has an atmosphere, but we couldn't breathe it. Air on Earth is mostly nitrogen and oxygen. Mars's atmosphere contains only small amounts of these gases. Instead, Martian air is almost all carbon dioxide gas. Carbon dioxide is poisonous to humans. The Martian atmosphere is only one-hundredth as thick as the Earth's. Atmospheres act like planetary blankets, keeping heat trapped near a planet's surface. One reason why Mars gets so cold is because it is wrapped in such a thin 'blanket'.

Ice Caps

Like the Earth, Mars has poles that are capped with ice (below). Mars's caps are not made simply of frozen water. Mars's north pole is covered in frozen carbon dioxide — what we call 'dry ice'. The southern ice cap is a combination of dry ice and frozen water.

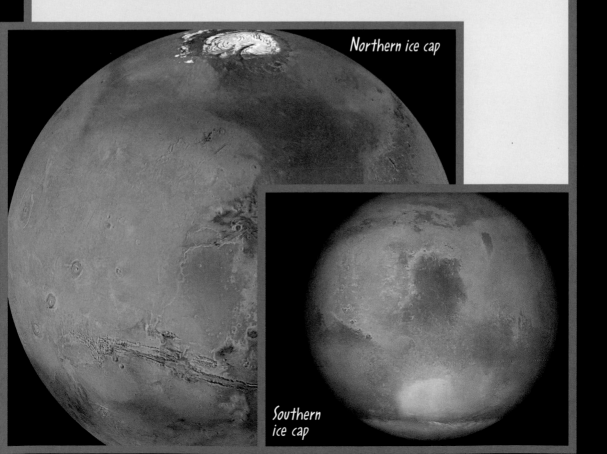

Northern ice cap

Southern
ice cap

As far as the eye can see, rocks and sand stretch out over the surface of a region of Mars. The boulders and sand are reddish because they contain a lot of rusted iron. Other areas of Mars have cliffs, canyons and towering volcanoes.

A Barren Wasteland

With no liquid water or plants, the surface of Mars looks like a wasteland. Sand dunes shift across broad plains. Impact craters – holes blasted open by the force of rocks falling from space – dot the landscape. Rocks thrown out of the craters lie scattered across the ground. Mars has deep canyons, jagged hills and steep cliffs. All of them are dry and nearly all of them are covered in red dust.

Giants Found on Mars!

Although Mars is a little planet, it does things big. The surface of Mars is covered with spectacular features.

Mars's biggest volcano, Olympus Mons, is more than 24,000 metres tall. That's almost three times as tall as the tallest mountain on Earth. The area it covers is about twice the size of Great Britain. Actually, Mars has several giant volcanoes that dwarf the tallest mountains that are found on Earth.

IT'S A FACT!
The Valles Marineris reaches 600 km wide and is 8 km deep in places.

At 277 miles long the Grand Canyon in the USA is the largest gorge on Earth. Mars has a gorge that is almost as long as the entire United States! It's called the Valles Marineris. It is almost 4,000 km (2,500 miles) from end to end. It looks like a gigantic scar slicing across the equator of Mars.

Olympus Mons (right) is the largest known volcano in the solar system. The volcano's opening is nearly 3 km (2 miles) deep and 100 km (60 miles) wide. The Valles Marineris (below) is another large feature of Mars.

Close-up of the Valles Marineris

Days and Years

A day is the time it takes for a planet to spin once on its axis. A year is the time it takes a planet to go once around the Sun. Each planet has its own length of day and year. A day on Mars is almost the same length as one day on Earth, but Mars's year is almost twice as long as the Earth's year. If you had grown up on Mars, you would have had about the same number of breakfasts but only half as many birthdays.

1,900 km (1,200 miles)

An ancient asteroid struck Mars, creating the huge impact crater Hellas Planitia (above).

What would happen if a rocky planet got hit by a huge asteroid. You would get something like Hellas Planitia, the largest impact crater on Mars. Hellas Planitia is more than 1,900 km (1,200 miles) across. That's nearly one and a half times the length of Britain! It is more than 10 km (6 miles) deep in places. A collision that powerful could have launched Martian rocks out into space! Scientists think this is maybe why pieces of Martian rock are sometimes found on Earth.

IT'S A FACT!

Enough rock and dust were thrown out of Hellas Planitia during the impact to bury the entire country of China 3 km (2 miles) deep.

chapter 2

Destination Mars

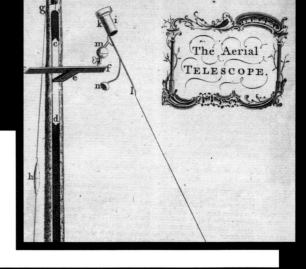

The Aerial TELESCOPE.

Mars is cold, dry and desolate. Why would we want to spend a lot of time exploring a dusty rock? Well, as harsh as Mars seems, no other planet or moon is as much like our own home. Many scientists think Mars is the most likely place to find life beyond Earth. It may also be the easiest place beyond Earth for humans to live.

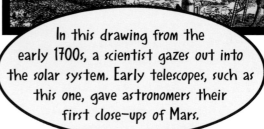

In this drawing from the early 1700s, a scientist gazes out into the solar system. Early telescopes, such as this one, gave astronomers their first close-ups of Mars.

The telescope was invented in the early 1600s. This new tool showed astronomers that Mars was much like the Earth. Some began to wonder if the planet might contain

Canals?

In the late 1800s, astronomer Percival Lowell (*below*) reported what he believed to be canals crisscrossing Mars (*right*). Where the canals intersected, he saw dark patches. He decided the dark patches were plants fed by water from the canals. Lowell concluded that the canals had been made by intelligent Martians. He thought the Martians were trying to irrigate their dry planet using water from Mars's ice caps. Lowell's ideas may sound far-fetched. At the time, though, many people thought he was right.

Lowell's canals, it turns out, were optical illusions. His telescope was not powerful enough to see surface features on Mars clearly. What he thought were lines actually were disconnected patches that happened to line up. The human brain is always looking for patterns. Sometimes our brains see patterns where none really exist.

life. Perhaps Mars, like Earth, was home to intelligent creatures. That was something no telescope was powerful enough to view. The question of life on Mars was left open to people's imaginations.

By the mid-1900s, books, movies, radio programmes and TV shows filled in what telescopes could not see. They created a fantasy Mars complete with monsters, spaceships and death rays.

Getting a Closer Look

Even with our best telescopes, we cannot see small features on the surface of Mars clearly. Mars is just too far away. Our best views of Mars have come from up close. For more than 40 years, we have been busy sending robots to Mars to explore its mysteries. However, this isn't as easy as it might seem. Of all the missions to Mars ever attempted, more than half have failed.

We think of planets as being large. Compared to the vastness of space, though, they're really quite small. Mars is only about 6,400 km (4,000 miles) wide. It rarely gets any closer than about 56 million km (35 million miles) to Earth. Mars is a very small target, very far away, and it's moving.

On a different scale, suppose you have a magnet the size of a speck of dust. Imagine also that you're travelling in a moving car. Now imagine you want to launch the speck-sized magnet from your moving car. Your goal is to stick it to the bumper of another moving car. However the other car never gets closer than about 40 km (25 miles) away.

The planets Venus (*below right*) and Mars (*below left*) appear as two small dots in the night sky. Planets are tiny compared to the vastness of space.

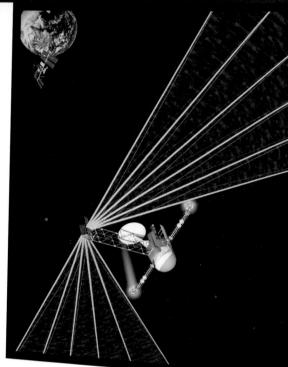

An artist's idea of what spacecraft leaving for Mars might look like. Flights to Mars take a lot of planning.

Let's also say it will take the magnet exactly six months to fly that far. If that's the case, you can't launch the magnet to where the other car is now. You need to aim it to where the car will be in exactly six months. That doesn't sound easy, does it?

Even when a mission's flight path is calculated just right, plenty else can go wrong. Thousands of parts have to work together perfectly for a mission to succeed. Once it is launched, there is no way to fix problems that develop. You can't pull over and get a mechanic to take a look. One tiny mistake and it's all over. All you can do is try again.

It takes space probes six to eight months to travel from the Earth to Mars. After the excitement of launch, scientists have lots of time to wait and to worry. Radio signals move at the speed of light, but because Mars is so far away, radio signals take 10 to 20 minutes to travel between Mars and Earth. When a space probe warns that it's in trouble, controllers on Earth get the message up to 20 minutes later. Any response controllers send will take just as long to get back. This means you can't help an endangered space probe in 'real time'. Imagine having to swerve to avoid a car accident 40 minutes before it's going to happen! Suspense is part of every mission.

Early Missions

In the 1960s, NASA – the National Aeronautics and Space Administration – launched the Mariner space probes. These probes gave us our first close look at the red planet.

Mariner 4 blasted off in November 1964. Its mission was to fly by Mars. It would give the world its first good look at the surface of Mars.

IT'S A FACT!

NASA is the space agency of the United States. Europe's version of NASA is the European Space Agency (ESA).

First Tries

The Soviet Union's *Marsnik 1* space probe was launched in October 1960. It was the world's first attempt to explore Mars using a robot. *Marsnik 1* never even got close. It crashed back to Earth after only 120 km (75 miles) of flight.

The United States' first try, *Mariner 3*, didn't fare any better. The probe launched successfully in November 1964. Unfortunately, a protective shield failed to come off as expected. With the shield stuck on, the probe was useless. The mission was over soon after it had started.

A scientist looks at one of the first close-range photographs of the surface of Mars (*above*). *Mariner 4* (*top*) took the image and 21 others in 1965.

On 15 July, 1965, *Mariner 4* flew its camera to within 10,000 km (6,200 miles) of the surface of Mars. NASA scientists cheered. Mission accomplished! As the first pictures came back, it became clear that the fantasy Mars did not match the reality. *Mariner 4* found no alien cities. It found only craters and red dust – a barren wasteland with no signs of life. The probe discovered that Mars's atmosphere is very thin. Living creatures would need a thicker atmosphere. Two more fly-bys in 1969 (*Mariners 6* and *7*) confirmed *Mariner 4*'s lifeless view of Mars.

Searching for Hidden Life – Viking 1 and Viking 2

Life as we know it cannot exist without water. Water makes up about 70 per cent of every living thing on Earth, from people to plants to single-celled creatures. The presence of water on a planet does not guarantee that life exists there. However, without water there is no chance of life as we know it. Pictures taken by the Mariner probes showed dry riverbeds on the surface of Mars. Had water once flowed there? Could some water still be there, under the ground? Perhaps Martians were there after all, but not the civilized kind. Perhaps there were tiny Martians. Maybe they were buried in the red soil, living on traces of water beneath the dry surface. The best way to tell would be to dig.

In the late summer of 1975, the Viking landers blasted off. They were NASA's first mission to touch down on another planet. The landers would test the soil for the presence of microbes – animals or plants too small to see without a microscope.

The First Mars Lander

In 1976, *Viking 1* gave us our first look around Mars from ground level. It was not the first lander to touch the Martian surface. Three Soviet landers each made it there earlier. *Mars 2* and *Mars 3* arrived in 1971. *Mars 6* landed in 1973. However, none of the three successfully sent back any information from the surface.

The Viking 1 lander (right) provided the first images of Mars from the surface. The lander took this image of the Martian landscape on 24 July, 1976.

The Face

In 1976, NASA released a *Viking 1* photograph of the surface of Mars that contained an interesting feature. It showed a rocky hill that seemed to be shaped like a human face (*right*). Most people who saw it thought it was nothing more than a coincidence. A few, though, concluded that the face was the work of aliens. Perhaps, they said, it was a monument left behind by some great Martian civilization.

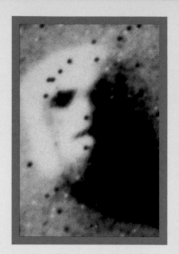

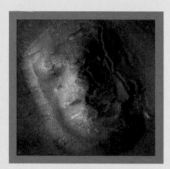

In 2001, *Mars Global Surveyor* took photographs of the same area. Its photographs were up to 100 times clearer than *Viking's*. It turns out that the feature is simply an oddly shaped hill (*left*). It doesn't look much like a face at all in the clearer pictures. Like Percival Lowell's canals, the face turned out to be fiction.

The landers sampled the soil, heated it and analysed it. Some results seemed promising at first, but in the end, each turned out to be a false hope. Mission scientists eventually concluded that the samples contained no sure evidence of life.

The Mariner and Viking missions failed to find proof of Martian life – past or present. They showed that nothing could survive on the surface. The conditions there are too extreme.

Not everyone gave up hope of finding life on Mars. More recent probes sent to Mars are changing our view of the red planet. These missions are revealing that Mars wasn't always a dusty wasteland.

Eyes in the Sky

In early 2006, four new orbiters cruised the skies above Mars. Each has added to our understanding of the planet.

Mars Global Surveyor took these pictures of surface rock on Mars. Some scientists believe the swirls, cracks and lumpy layers were created by water long ago.

Mars Global Surveyor (MGS) has been orbiting Mars since September 1997. It has mapped every bit of the surface of Mars. MGS's camera is able to pick out surface features as small as a van. That's up to 100 times clearer than any previous orbiter could see! MGS photographs are giving scientists a look into the planet's past.

Some photographs show what appear to be dried-out ponds and lakes. Other images show gullies carved into cliffs. The gullies look like they were created by moving water.

Mars Global Surveyor has also been able to measure the planet's magnetic field. It turns out that unlike the Earth, Mars does not have magnetic poles. So if you're planning on going to Mars, don't bother to bring your compass. It won't work.

Mars Odyssey has been studying Mars up close since October 2001. *Odyssey* is designed to work out what makes up the crust of Mars. *Odyssey* has made maps of where certain chemicals are found. From this information, scientists know that Mars has lots of frozen water underground near the poles.

Odyssey has also measured how much radiation a person would be exposed to on the planet. Dangerous types of radiation from the Sun can travel straight through the thin atmosphere of Mars.

In 2003, the European Space Agency successfully launched *Mars Express*. This was ESA's first attempt at exploring another planet. *Express* was designed to take very clear 3-D photographs of Mars and look for signs of water down to a few kilometres beneath the surface of Mars.

In this computer image, *Odyssey* flies over the north polar ice cap on Mars. The picture will appear in three dimensions when viewed through 3-D glasses.

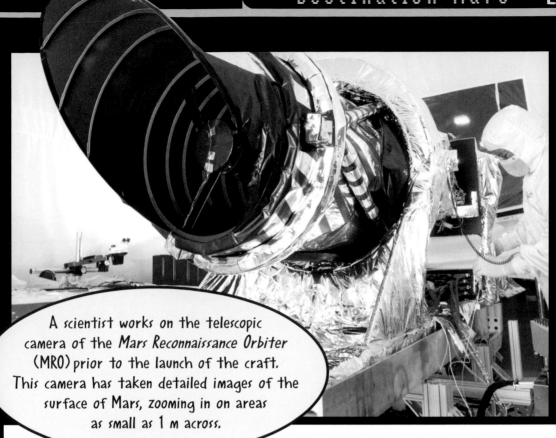

A scientist works on the telescopic camera of the *Mars Reconnaissance Orbiter* (MRO) prior to the launch of the craft. This camera has taken detailed images of the surface of Mars, zooming in on areas as small as 1 m across.

The UK-built lander *Beagle 2* was launched from *Mars Express* in 2003 to examine the rocks and soil of Mars. Unfortunately, the mission failed because *Beagle 2* was believed to have hit the planets surface too hard when landing and was badly damaged.

Mars Express has already made some important discoveries. Its high-resolution stereo camera has sent back stunning photographs of the planet. Scientists are examining landscapes of deep valleys, probably formed by glaciers. Any surface water has disappeared.

The Mars Reconnaissance Orbiter (MRO) arrived at Mars in March 2006. MRO carries with it the latest instruments to study the surface of Mars. MRO's camera can pick out objects as small as a dinner table. It can also make maps of surface chemicals in finer detail than ever before. MRO will help scientists pick the best sites for future landers to explore.

For studying Martian rocks, nothing beats being there. Enter *Spirit* and *Opportunity,* rolling robot geologists. *Spirit* and *Opportunity* are Mars Exploration Rovers (MERs). They are like radio-controlled cars packed with tools for studying Martian rocks and soil. The rovers' mission is to hunt for signs of water. Water leaves its mark wherever it has been. If Mars once was wet, it should be written in the rocks.

The rovers bring along a treasure chest of technology. Each MER is equipped with a panoramic camera (Pancam). Pancam is a two-eyed periscope for scanning the surrounding terrain. Because it has two eyes, Pancam can see the Martian surface in 3-D. Using Pancam, the rovers can identify hazards. This helps them move safely from place to place.

An extendable robot arm is mounted on the front of each rover. A microscope, a camera, a rock-scraping tool and chemical sensors are all part of the arm. Each rover carries a device for detecting heat given off by rocks and soil. Power comes from solar panels that convert sunlight into electricity.

Landing an MER

Most landers have retro-rockets. A lander aims these rocket engines at the ground to slow its descent. That way, the lander doesn't crash when it lands. To save fuel, weight and money, the Mars Exploration Rovers were packed inside inflatable cushions (airbags) instead. *Spirit* and *Opportunity* were designed to land with a bounce.

NASA used airbags (above) to cushion the landings of Spirit and Opportunity on Mars.

All this equipment sits on top of an insect-like machine with six multipurpose wheels. Each wheel can move independently. This flexibility allows the rovers to move over rocks and holes without tipping over. The wheels can even be used to dig trenches.

IT'S A FACT!
Opportunity and *Spirit* weren't the first rovers on Mars. A rover named *Sojourner* explored a little patch of Mars in 1997.

Each rover is about the size of a golf buggy. To save space during the trip to Mars, all that equipment was folded up tightly. When folded, each rover was not much bigger than a microwave oven. Once they were safe on the ground, the rovers unfolded like high-tech Transformers.

The Pancam of an MER is a periscope-camera (left centre) that can pan (turn) to view its surroundings. Pancams have two lenses that allow MERs to take 3-D pictures.

Spirit and *Opportunity* landed on opposite sides of Mars in January 2004. Both landed in areas scientists thought might have signs of water. Although *Spirit* was the first to land, *Opportunity* was the first rover to hit the jackpot.

By chance, *Opportunity* landed at the bottom of a small impact crater. Bedrock – the solid layer of rock that lies under the soil – was exposed within the crater. Within the bedrock, *Opportunity* found signs of water. To mission scientists, it was a planetary hole in one!

A pattern called cross-bedding was visible within the rocks. On Earth, cross-beds can form when sand is pushed by a current of water. In among the cross-beds, *Opportunity* saw small spheres the size of ball bearings. Scientists called the spheres blueberries. Analysis of the blueberries showed they were made of hematite – a mineral we commonly call rust. On Earth, rust balls like this form in rocks soaked with water.

Opportunity found even more evidence of water. The rover detected large amounts of salt minerals in the rocks. On Earth, deposits like these form only in the presence of water. They form either in standing water or in rock with lots of water flowing through it. Without a doubt, *Opportunity*'s landing site was once wet.

Spirit, on the other hand, toiled away for more than six months without finding much evidence of water. Everything changed, though, when the rover began its climb into the Columbia Hills. These hills are high ground a little more than 3 km (2 miles) from *Spirit*'s landing site.

Columbia Station

Rover scientists named *Spirit*'s landing site Columbia Station and the nearby hills the Columbia Hills. The names honour the seven astronauts who died when the space shuttle *Columbia* exploded on 1 February, 2003. The first of the hills *Spirit* climbed was named Husband Hill in honour of Rick Husband, *Columbia*'s commander.

Spirit photographs its climb up the Columbia Hills (far left). The rover found altered rock (left) there, which suggests that water was once present.

The Great Martian Salt Lake?

What kind of a world was Mars back in its 'wet' days? Despite the water, it probably wasn't all that nice. The salt minerals *Opportunity* found form in acidic water. Strong acid destroys human skin. The water probably wasn't very deep, either. Scientists think *Opportunity*'s landing site probably was wet only sometimes. In between, it dried out, leaving salt minerals behind. So, instead of oceans of refreshing water, think shallow lakes of acid.

Staring upwards like a giant eye, Eagle Crater (left) may have been the site of a salty lake. Meridiani Planum (right) may also have once been a salt lake.

What *Spirit* found there was altered rock. The rock had been changed from hard and strong to soft and weak. When this happens to rocks on Earth, water is usually the cause. Then, in February 2005, *Spirit* discovered a rock containing high amounts of sulphur salt. This kind of chemical typically forms when water seeps through rocks. It takes a lot of water to leave behind a lot of salt minerals. So, at some point, the rocks of the Columbia Hills had got very wet.

Global Surveyor, Odyssey, Express and the rovers have all found good evidence that Mars was once a wet planet, but when was it wet? No one can say exactly. Scientists are sure it was a very long time ago. Perhaps it was even billions of years ago. That doesn't mean that the planet is dry and dead underneath. Future orbiters and landers are set to find out.

chapter 3

Future Missions to Mars

NASA has committed to exploring the red planet. The American space agency hopes to launch a new mission to Mars every 26 months for the next decade. Each mission will have special abilities and goals. Their shared purpose is to 'follow the water'. Water is the common link connecting everything scientists want to investigate.

Phoenix Scout

In August 2007, NASA launched *Phoenix*, the first mission in its Scout programme. The Scout missions are smaller and less expensive than previous missions. NASA hopes to send a variety of Scouts to Mars over the next couple of decades.

Phoenix Scout is a stationary lander. It is due to touch down near the north pole of Mars in May 2008. *Phoenix* will try to sample the underground ice *Mars Odyssey* found. The lander will use a long, robotic arm

An artist's illustration of the *Phoenix* lander. The lander is equipped to collect and analyse soil, rock and ice samples at the north polar cap of Mars.

to dig holes up to 0.5 m deep. *Phoenix* will also be able to collect and study soil samples. Similar to the MERs, *Phoenix* has a two-eyed periscope for a 3-D examination of its surroundings.

MTO: Victim of the Money Crunch

Without money, no Mars mission can ever succeed. Sending even one probe to Mars costs billions of pounds. Sometimes a good idea dies because of a lack of money. *Mars Telecommunications Orbiter* (MTO) was scheduled to be launched in September 2009. MTO was to act as a communications link between the Earth and Mars. Every Mars spacecraft needs to communicate with scientists on Earth. With more missions on the way, more information will need to be sent back and forth. Scientists hoped MTO would make communication between the planets faster and better. As good as that sounds, it's now not going to happen. Budget cuts in 2005 forced NASA to cut the MTO programme.

Mars Science Laboratory (MSL)

Getting ready for a late 2009 launch is the *Mars Science Laboratory*. This will be the biggest and most versatile Mars rover yet. MSL will be the first Mars spacecraft able to steer itself to its landing site. The rest just landed wherever they fell.

While on the red planet, MSL will study rocks, soil and the atmosphere. It will look for water and signs of life. This rover will really get around. MSL should be able to drive as far as 19 km (12 miles) from its landing site.

Although run by NASA, *Mars Science Laboratory* will be an international machine. Russia, Spain, Canada and Germany all plan to contribute scientific instruments for the rover.

Exploring Mars Beyond 2009

What about beyond 2009? Scientists and engineers are already hard at work on the future. They aren't just creating fancier orbiters, landers and rovers. Instead, they are experimenting with new ways of exploring the planet. They are even planning ways to bring pieces of Mars back home.

MSL (above) is designed to be a mobile science lab. Its mission will include looking for water and evidence of life on Mars, as well as studying the atmosphere.

Flying on Mars: Inflatable Aeroplane Wings

Aeroplanes on Mars won't be like those on Earth. Normal aeroplanes aren't the right shape to fit on a rocket. The wings stick out much too far. Aeroplanes that go to Mars will need to travel small. One solution is to have wings that inflate like balloons. These aeroplanes will arrive in Mars's orbit with their wings tucked away. Then, as they fall towards the surface, the wings will inflate. With their wings in place, the Marsplanes will be free to soar.

This is one design for a Mars exploration aircraft. Scientists on Earth will fly these planes by remote control. The trick? Getting the planes to fit onto a rocket.

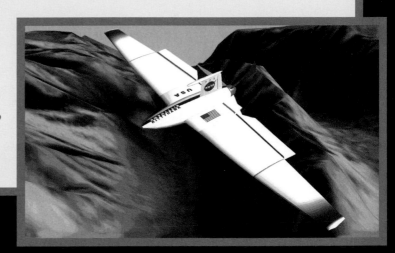

The next Scout may be another lander or rover. It may also be something completely different. Engineers are designing remote-controlled aeroplanes for Mars exploration. Other scientists are designing balloons that can drift around the planet. Others are busy creating 'tumbleweed rovers'. Tumbleweed rovers will use wind power to roll from place to place across the surface of the planet.

These new designs will never replace the tried-and-tested methods of the past. Yet they all have advantages over previous Mars machines. Aeroplanes and balloons can take a closer look than any orbiter. They can cover more territory than any rover. Tumbleweeds weigh less and cost less than traditional rovers. That means more robots could be sent at one time.

Any life or liquid water on Mars is most likely to be found underground. We may have to dig tens or even hundreds of metres to find it. Some scientists hope to send rovers equipped with drills that can probe that deep. NASA is also working on designs for a robotic 'mole'. This device will drill itself into the ground to sample soil or ice.

Studying a rock from millions of miles away is never as useful as looking at it with your own two eyes. If we could bring Mars rocks back to Earth, we could get our best look at them yet. In 2014 and again in 2016, NASA hopes to launch missions to do just that. Using rovers or landers, scientists plan to collect rocks and soil they want to study. The samples will then go into sample return capsules. Safe inside the capsules, they will blast off Mars and head for Earth.

IT'S A FACT!
Launching a mission when your space probe has the shortest distance to travel saves time, fuel and money. This ideal time for launching a space mission is known as the launch window. For Mars, the launch window comes around every 26 months.

In this concept painting, a sample return capsule blasts off for Earth. Sample return capsules could get samples of Mars into the hands of eager scientists on Earth. Mole landers may drill for pockets of Martian water deep in the ground (inset).

chapter 4

Life on Mars

When the first probes travelled to Mars in the 1960s, scientists were looking for life on or just under the planet's surface. Since then, life has been found on Earth in the most unlikely places. Deep, dark, toxic places. Extreme places. Perhaps Martian microbes could be living where no one has looked for them before.

Living in Acid

Acid kills – strong acid does, anyway. Biologists have long thought that nothing could live in strongly acidic water. The Mars Analog Research and Technology Experiment (MARTE) showed that some things can.

These rock-eating bacteria (*red*) really eat rock (*green*). They were discovered more than 0.8 km (0.5 mile) inside Earth. Similar kinds of bacteria might exist in deep Martian rock.

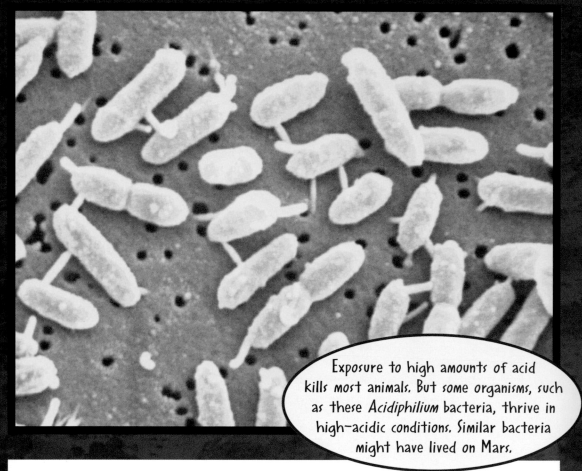

Exposure to high amounts of acid kills most animals. But some organisms, such as these *Acidiphilium* bacteria, thrive in high-acidic conditions. Similar bacteria might have lived on Mars.

In 2003 and 2004, MARTE scientists tested to see how robots could be used to drill for life on Mars. They used robots to drill in an extreme environment here on Earth. Near Rio Tinto, Spain, the MARTE team found microbes living in strongly acidic water. If some microbes on Earth can live in strong acid, maybe microbes have lived that way on Mars, and maybe they still do.

Still Life

When an animal freezes solid, you can almost always be sure that it's dead. Why? Freezing kills cells. Frozen cells cannot function and usually burst. However, new evidence suggests this isn't always true. Some types of life can survive even if they're frozen for a very long time.

In 2000, NASA's Richard Hoover discovered bacteria frozen within underground ice in Alaska. The ice had been frozen solid for 30,000 years – since the middle of the Ice Age. When Hoover melted the ice, the bacteria immediately began to swim. They acted as if no time had passed since the ice had first frozen.

What does this mean for Mars? If life did exist on Mars, it might be frozen in the ice. Future explorers may be able to thaw ice on Mars and find something swimming around.

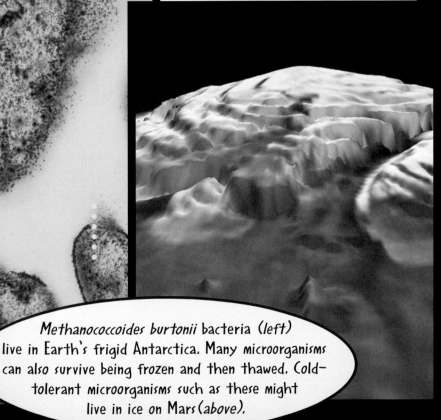

Methanococcoides burtonii bacteria (left) live in Earth's frigid Antarctica. Many microorganisms can also survive being frozen and then thawed. Cold-tolerant microorganisms such as these might live in ice on Mars (above).

This artist's illustration shows *Mars Express* above the Martian atmosphere. The craft has detected high amounts of methane — a possible sign of life — in the planet's atmosphere.

Evidence from the Air

The latest evidence of life on Mars has come not from rocks or soil but from the air. In 2004, *Mars Express* detected significant amounts of methane in the atmosphere of Mars. This is important because methane is a kind of natural gas that living things can produce. The methane could instead be from some other source, such as volcanoes. No one is totally sure. More research is under way.

Martian Meteorite ALH84001

Surprisingly, some of the most exciting evidence for life on Mars has come from a rock found on Earth. In 1993, researchers studied a meteorite that they called ALH84001. They discovered that it had gases within it. The gases matched the atmosphere of Mars. The scientists concluded that the rock must have come from Mars. The rock probably was thrown into space many years ago, when an asteroid collided with Mars. Inside the rock were shapes that looked a lot like bacteria fossils.

IT'S A FACT!

A meteorite is a rock from space that lands on Earth.

Had evidence of life on Mars finally been found?

The findings were finally announced in 1996. The story was all over the news. The researchers said they were confident the meteorite was a sign of life on Mars.

Not everyone was convinced. Some scientists said the shapes might have formed in some other way. The shapes' match with bacteria was a coincidence, they said. Others thought the shapes could have formed not on Mars but on Earth, after the rock landed.

After even more research, scientists still do not agree about it. Mars itself may have to cast the deciding vote.

Some scientists think life could have been carried to Earth on meteorites. ALH84001 (right) is a meteorite that came from Mars. It may contain microscopic fossils of ancient bacteria (yellow) from Mars.

ALH84001,0

0.4"
(1 cm)

Earth Life on Mars?

If life is found on Mars, scientists will first have to make sure it really is Martian life. Another possibility is that microbes from Earth may have found their way to Mars.

In 1972, *Apollo 12* astronauts brought a camera back from the Moon. It had been sent there three years earlier by the *Surveyor 3* spacecraft. When the camera was studied back on Earth, scientists found bacteria in the camera. The bacteria had been in there the entire time the camera was on the Moon – and they were alive! The bacteria had survived without air, food or protection from radiation. They had survived temperatures colder than –240°C.

US astronaut Charles Conrad Jr examines *Surveyor 3* during the 1972 *Apollo 12* mission to the Moon. The astronauts brought back a camera from *Surveyor*. It contained living Earth bacteria that had survived three years without air or water.

The conditions those microbes endured are pretty similar to conditions in space. Imagine if microbes were on a lander before it left Earth. They might survive the trip through space from Earth to Mars! Microbes carried from Earth could end up in Martian rock or soil samples. They could give scientists the false impression that Martian life had been found.

Some scientists think that microbes from Earth could have gone to Mars long ago. They could have been transported on meteorites flung off our planet by asteroid impacts. Deposited on Mars, they might have made the planet their new home. If these scientists are right, Earthlings may have invaded Mars long ago!

chapter 5

People on Mars

On 21 July, 1969, Neil Armstrong uttered the famous words: 'That's one small step for man, one giant leap for mankind'. He had just taken his first step onto the surface of the moon. Now, forty years later, humans are setting their sights on the red planet. With the developments of technology in recent years, the stage has been set for humans to take their first steps on Mars in the not-too-distant future.

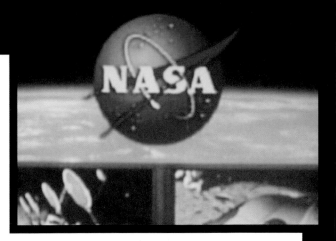

Apollo 11 astronaut Edwin Aldrin photographed this footprint as part of an experiment to study the nature of dust on the moon.

In theory, getting people to Mars is no more difficult than getting rovers to Mars. But of course, simply getting them there is not the point. The goal is to get them there *alive*, keep them alive while on Mars and get them back home safely. Unlike a spacecraft, people need food, water and shelter. People need to move and exercise to stay healthy. People need air to breathe. All these needs – and many more – must be taken care of during the entire trip.

The distance between Earth and Mars is always changing. People who make it to Mars will not be able to turn around and come straight home. They will have to wait for the planets to line up correctly before they can return. After the trip to Mars, the astronauts may have to wait there for a further 18 months. Packing enough supplies for even one person to be gone that long will be a difficult task.

A scientist experiences what life on Mars might be like at the Mars Desert Research Station in Utah, USA. In addition to spacesuits, astronauts on Mars will need shelter (*in background*), water and food.

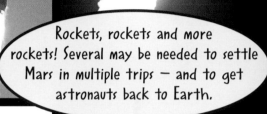

Rockets, rockets and more rockets! Several may be needed to settle Mars in multiple trips — and to get astronauts back to Earth.

An even bigger problem will be fuel. To return home, astronauts will need to be able to blast off from Mars. Launching a rocket into space takes tremendous amounts of fuel. The rocket has to fight the pull of gravity. That's hard work! You could carry extra fuel from Earth and save it for later, but that could be a problem. Fuel is heavy and dangerous.

At least one plan, Mars Direct, has an answer to the fuel problem. The idea is that the astronauts wouldn't take everything to Mars in one huge rocket. Instead, multiple rockets would be launched over several years.

Marsquakes?

Long thought to be stable, Mars may still shake a little after all. Some features on Mars look like they were formed by recent quakes. The quakes may have occurred in the last 10 or 20 years. Why is that important? If we do send humans to Mars, we need to know if they have to be prepared for quakes. An unexpected Marsquake could damage important equipment. People might get hurt. Millions of miles away from help, such accidents would cause a lot of problems.

In year one, for example, a rocket carrying the Earth Return Vehicle (ERV) goes to Mars. Once on Mars, the ERV deploys a machine. The machine can make rocket fuel from chemicals in the atmosphere. Instead of carrying fuel for the return trip, the ERV makes its own! The next Mars launch window comes 26 months later. This is when the astronauts head for Mars. The astronauts land near the ERV and spend 18 months studying the planet. They then head home on the ERV. By then, the ERV has made enough fuel for the return trip.

Making Ourselves at Home

One day we may decide to set up a permanent human colony on Mars. If we do, we may find that the settlers get tired of having to walk around in spacesuits. They might decide they would like Mars to be more like their warm, comfortable home planet. The settlers might try terraforming Mars – changing Mars to become more like Earth.

This artist's illustration shows what an early colony on Mars might look like.

The Greenhouse Effect

Greenhouses (right) keep plants warm in winter by letting sunlight in and trapping the heat inside. Atmospheres keep planets warm in a similar way. The atmosphere traps heat near the planet and stops it from escaping. This is called the greenhouse effect. On Earth, where temperatures are already comfortable, increasing the planet's greenhouse effect is a bad thing. On Mars, though, a little global warming might feel quite good.

Some scientists think we could warm up Mars by giving it a greater greenhouse effect. How could we do it? Certain gases are especially good at trapping heat. Carbon dioxide – the gas that makes up most of the atmosphere of Mars – is one of them. Certain human-made gases are even better. People could release greenhouse gases such as these into the atmosphere, causing the planet to begin warming up.

Once the planet is warmer, plants could be brought to live there. Plants take in carbon dioxide and give off oxygen. People need oxygen to breathe. Over time, the plants would replace carbon dioxide in the atmosphere of Mars with oxygen. This process would probably take many years – perhaps even thousands. But in theory, it could make the air on Mars breathable by humans.

A question that is perhaps more important than 'Can we terraform Mars?' is 'If we can, is it right to do it?' Some people argue that if Mars does have living things of its own, we have no right to change their habitat to make it the way we like it. After all, we already have a planet of our own.

Some people worry that we might not be able to keep control of a terraforming experiment. Global warming might not go as planned. The planet's weather might become unstable and unpredictable. Humans are having problems keeping our own planet healthy. Should we be trusted to play around with another one?

Will Mars be turned into another Earth? Stay tuned. The Earthling invasion of Mars is already in progress.

This image shows what a terraformed Mars might look like, with liquid water, vegetation and a breathable atmosphere.

Glossary

asteroids: large space rocks that orbit the Sun but are smaller than planets

atmosphere: the layer of gases that surrounds a planet

bacteria: single-celled organisms

dry ice: frozen carbon dioxide

gravity: the force that pulls objects towards the centre of a planet

lander: a robotic space probe that does not move from its landing site

launch window: the period of time during which a spacecraft must be launched to get to its destination

meteorite: a small rock from space that lands on Earth

microbes: tiny organisms that can be seen only with a microscope

orbiter: a spacecraft designed to stay in orbit around a planet

probe: a craft used to explore space

radar: a device that sends out radio waves and picks them up again after they bounce off objects

rover: a robotic lander that can travel away from its landing site

terraform: to change a planet to make it more like Earth

Selected Bibliography

Coffin, Rick. *WhatonMars.com*. 2006. http://www.whatonmars.com (25 April 2006).

European Space Agency. *Mars Express*. 2006. http://www.esa.int/export/SPECIALS/Mars _Express/ (25 April 2006).

Imaginova. *SPACE.com*. 2006. http://www.space.com (25 April 2006).

Lowell, Percival. *Mars*. 2006. http://www.wanderer.org/references/lowell/Mars/ (25 April 2006).

Lowell Observatory. 'Percival Lowell'. *About Lowell Observatory*. 2006. http://www.lowell.edu/AboutLowell/plowell.html (25 April 2006).

Malin Space Science Systems. *The 'Face on Mars'*. 2006. http://barsoom.msss.com/education/facepage/face.html (25 April 2006).

NASA. *Mars Exploration Rover Mission*. 2006. http://marsrovers.jpl.nasa.gov/home/index.html (25 April 2006).

NASA. 'Mars Exploration Timeline'. 2006. http://nssdc.gsfc.nasa.gov/planetary/chronology_mars.html (25 April 2006).

NASA. *Mars Global Surveyor*. 2006. http://mars.jpl.nasa.gov/mgs/index.html (25 April 2006).

NASA. *Mars Odyssey*. 2005. http://mars3.jpl.nasa.gov/odyssey/ (14 February 2006).

NASA. *Mars Pathfinder Home*. 2005. http://mars.jpl.nasa.gov/MPF/index1.html (14 February 2006).

NASA. *Mars Reconnaissance Orbiter*. 2006. http://mars3.jpl.nasa.gov/mro/ (April 2006).

Further Reading and Websites

Bergin, Mark. *Exploration of Mars* (Accelerate) Book House, 2002.

Bond, Peter. *DK Guide to Space* (DK Guides) Dorling Kindersley Publishers Ltd, 2004.

Bradbury, Ray. *The Martian Chronicles* Voyager, 2001.

Goss, Tim. *Mars* (The Universe) Heinemann Library, 2008.

Mars (Eyewitness Guide) Dorling Kindersley Publishers Ltd, 2004.

Sparrow, Giles. *Mars* (Exploring the Solar System) Heinemann Library, 2002.

Wells, H G. *War of the Worlds*. 1898. Reprint. Penguin Classics; New Ed edition 2005

Winner, Cherie. *Life on the Edge* Lerner Books, 2008.

BBC: Science and Nature – Mars
http://www.bbc.co.uk/science/space/solarsystem/mars/
This website has detailed information on Mars as well as links to pages on all the other planets in the solar system.

Index

Photo Acknowledgements

The images in this book are used with the permission of: NASA-JPL, pp 1, 2 (background), 4 (background), 6 (both), 8 (background), 9 (both), 10 (both), 11 (all), 12 (both), 14 (background), 16 (all), 18 (all), 19, 20 (background and left), 21 (all), 22 (both), 23, 24 (background), 26 (all), 27 (all), 28 (background), 29, 30 (all), 32 (background and main), 34 (background), 35 (right), 36 (both), 37 (inset), 38 (background), 40 (background), 42 (background), 44 (background), 46 (background), 48 (background); © CORBIS, p 5; © NASA/JPL/Malin Space Science Systems, pp 7, 31; © PhotoDisc/Getty Images, p 8; NASA-GSFC, p 11 (main); © Hulton Archive/Getty Images, p 13; © SPL/Photo Researchers, Inc., pp 14 (top) 33; Library of Congress (LC-USZ62-128068), p 14 (bottom); NASA-JSC, pp 15, 38; NASA-MSFC, pp 16 (left and right), 42; © 1989 Roger Ressmeyer/NASA/CORBIS, p 20 (right); © NASA/JPL/ZUMA/CORBIS, p 24; © NASA/JPL/CORNELL/AFP/Getty Images, p 25; © Detlev van Ravenswaay/Photo Researchers, Inc., pp 32 (inset), 44; © James King-Holmes/Photo Researchers, Inc., p 34; © Dr M Rohde, GBF/Photo Researchers, Inc., p 35 (left); © Lynette Cook/Photo Researchers, Inc., p 37 (main); © Mark Wilson/Getty Images, pp 39 (top), 41 (right); © NASA/Discovery Photo Library 39 (bottom); © George Frey/Getty Images, pp 40, 43; © Matt Stroshane/Getty Images, p 41 (left and second right); NASA-KSC, p 41 (second left).Front cover: NASA-JPL (background, bottom left, top and bottom right); © Reuters/CORBIS (top left). Back cover: NASA-JPL (background).

This book was first published in the United States of America in 2007.
Text copyright © 2007 by David J Ward

About the Author

David Ward teaches astronomy, physics and geology. He is married and has two sons. He enjoys walking, cycling and playing basketball.